797,885 Books
are available to read at

Forgotten Books

www.ForgottenBooks.com

Forgotten Books' App
Available for mobile, tablet & eReader

ISBN 978-1-331-50026-1
PIBN 10198527

This book is a reproduction of an important historical work. Forgotten Books uses state-of-the-art technology to digitally reconstruct the work, preserving the original format whilst repairing imperfections present in the aged copy. In rare cases, an imperfection in the original, such as a blemish or missing page, may be replicated in our edition. We do, however, repair the vast majority of imperfections successfully; any imperfections that remain are intentionally left to preserve the state of such historical works.

Forgotten Books is a registered trademark of FB &c Ltd.
Copyright © 2017 FB &c Ltd.
FB &c Ltd, Dalton House, 60 Windsor Avenue, London, SW19 2RR.
Company number 08720141. Registered in England and Wales.

For support please visit www.forgottenbooks.com

1 MONTH OF FREE READING

at

www.ForgottenBooks.com

By purchasing this book you are eligible for one month membership to ForgottenBooks.com, giving you unlimited access to our entire collection of over 700,000 titles via our web site and mobile apps.

To claim your free month visit: www.forgottenbooks.com/free198527

* Offer is valid for 45 days from date of purchase. Terms and conditions apply.

English
Français
Deutsche
Italiano
Español
Português

www.forgottenbooks.com

Mythology Photography **Fiction** Fishing Christianity **Art** Cooking Essays **Buddhism** Freemasonry Medicine **Biology** Music **Ancient Egypt** Evolution Carpentry Physics Dance Geology **Mathematics** Fitness Shakespeare **Folklore** Yoga Marketing **Confidence** Immortality Biographies Poetry **Psychology** Witchcraft Electronics Chemistry History **Law** Accounting **Philosophy** Anthropology Alchemy Drama Quantum Mechanics Atheism Sexual Health **Ancient History** **Entrepreneurship** Languages Sport Paleontology Needlework Islam **Metaphysics** Investment Archaeology Parenting Statistics Criminology **Motivational**

An Important Communication *to the* friends *of the* New Hampshire Society *of the* Cincinnati

Cincinnati Memorial Hall Library and Military Museum
at
EXETER, NEW HAMPSHIRE

IN the year 1783, after a conflict of eight years, General Washington and his brother officers founded the Society of the Cincinnati to preserve inviolate the exalted rights and liberties for which they had fought and bled, to promote national union and national honor, and to render permanent the cordial affection and brotherly kindness towards one another, which should ever dwell in the hearts of those who have a common heritage. Thus as Washington, Knox, Hamilton, Pinckney, and other illustrious characters were among the founders of the Republic they were also the founders of the Cincinnati. Many of these distinguished Americans have memorials, but there has never been one dedicated to them as Cincinnati collectively, and to the Continental Army, until the founding of the Cincinnati Memorial Hall at Exeter, New Hampshire.

It is the purpose of the Society to make the Hall an object lesson to this and future generations, to teach the true meaning of the patriotic self-sacrifice, devotion and utter unselfishness of the men of the Revolution who fought for the welfare of mankind in the establishment of American Independence, by accumulating a library and collecting relics relating to them and the period.

In drawing your respectful attention to the Hall the Society does so in the belief that the patriotic, useful and instructive object of the enterprise will appeal to you strongly, as one having the interest of his country at heart, and, furthermore, the members of the New Hampshire Society feel that you will be honored by this opportunity to assist in such a laudable purpose, by having your name permanently identified with the work of this illustrious Order.

In order to properly equip, furnish and maintain the Hall as a museum and library it will be necessary to obtain subscriptions to a goodly amount, and there is now open to the friends of the Cincinnati an opportunity to perform an important share in the permanent establishment of the Hall.

Funds are also needed immediately to enable the Committee to proceed with certain necessary improvements, such as providing suitable quarters for a caretaker in order that the house proper may be devoted entirely to the use of the Society, and kept open for public inspection throughout the year.

The names of contributors will be inscribed upon a bronze tablet to be placed in the Hall.

It is also proposed to furnish the house, as far as possible, with genuine Colonial furniture, and donations of relics, family portraits, genealogical and historical books, documents, etc., will be greatly appreciated and carefully preserved. At present all such donations will be placed in a room in the Phillips Exeter Academy, through the courtesy of the trustees, until the house can be properly prepared for occupation by the Society.

FREDERICK BACON PHILBROOK,
Secretary.

THE OLD GILMAN HOUSE.
Front-end view.

Cincinnati Memorial Hall

AND

Military Museum

1783

EXETER, NEW HAMPSHIRE

FOR MANY YEARS KNOWN AS

The Gilman House
Built 1721

NOW OWNED BY THE

SOCIETY OF THE CINCINNATI

IN THE

STATE OF NEW HAMPSHIRE

1903

P.
Author.
11 Je '04

The Heintzemann Press Boston

The Purchase of the Gilman House
By the New Hampshire Society of the Cincinnati

THE usefulness and appropriateness of permanent headquarters for the Society became very apparent some few years ago, and a movement to purchase for such a purpose the historical house in Exeter known as the "Gilman House," was begun soon after the annual meeting of July 4, 1902.

A committee consisting of the President, Secretary and Treasurer, was appointed, with full powers, and within a few months sufficient funds were subscribed to enable the committee to purchase the property, the title to the estate passing to the Society, subject to a short lease, on November 1, 1902.

The necessity of a permanent residence and headquarters is threefold, viz.:

1. To provide an open house, where the members of the Society can go at any time they may desire, and moreover, so that all may feel that the Society has a permanent domicile. Further, to have an historic place in which to hold our commemorative meetings, and a safe depository for our valuable genealogical records, documents and papers, which is a matter of great importance.

2. To establish an ancestral hall and museum of historical relics and curios of the Colonial and Revolutionary periods, especially such as pertain to the New Hampshire Cincinnati, its original members and their families, and the officers of the New Hampshire Continental Line generally, which it is proposed to have open to the public. Also to establish a library of historical and genealogical books, documents and manuscripts pertaining to the history of New Hamphire in particular.

3. By maintaining some definite Society house as its permanent home, no greater security in perpetuating the New Hampshire Society and the remembrance of our ancestors' services in the War of the Revolution could be obtained.

Donations to the Hall and Museum

THE Committee respectfully solicits of all persons interested in the Colonial military history of the country, and of New Hampshire in particular, donations for the Hall and Military Museum and Library, of Colonial furniture, portraits, engravings, books, documents and relics, including Colonial firearms and side-arms, military uniforms and equipments, flags, medals, etc.

All will be carefully recorded in catalogue form and placed in a room at the Phillips Exeter Academy, which has been courteously extended for the purpose by the Trustees of that institution until final arrangements and furnishings can be completed for the occupancy of the Hall by the Society.

Any person, whether a member of the Society, an Annual Subscriber, or otherwise interested in perpetuating the honored memories of the patriots of the Revolution, may establish special funds, the whole or the interest from which to be devoted to general use or some specific purpose consistent with the objects of the Cincinnati and of the Memorial Hall.

All communications relating to Memorial Hall should be addressed to the President or the Secretary of the Society, at Exeter.

Form of Bequest

I give and bequeath to the New Hampshire Society of the Cincinnati, a corporation established by law in the State of New Hampshire, the sum of   dollars.

LIBRARY IN THE OLD GILMAN HOUSE.
From photograph taken in 1899.

1721 *The Gilman House* 1903

THE MOST HISTORIC MANSION IN THE STATE OF NEW HAMPSHIRE RELATING TO THE WAR OF THE REVOLUTION
By Frederick Bacon Philbrook

1721–1747

SITUATED on a slight elevation on "Governor's Lane," leading from and a few rods south of Water Street, in the old part of the historic town of Exeter, Rockingham County, New Hampshire, is the famous old homestead erected by Nathaniel Ladd in 1721. The lot has a frontage on Water Street of about two hundred feet and is a part of the original lot purchased of Eliphalet Coffin in the year above mentioned. The estate was retained in the possession of the Ladd family, being deeded to the sons of Nathaniel Ladd in 1738 and 1743, until 1747, when it was purchased and occupied by Colonel Daniel Gilman, a prominent townsman and the father of Colonel Nicholas Gilman, Sr.

1752

In 1752, Colonel Nicholas Gilman, Sr., then twenty-one years of age, brought his bride of twenty to the house and here they resided for thirty-one years and until their deaths, which occurred within a few weeks of each other, in 1783. Here their children were born, and it was during Colonel Gilman's occupancy of the house that the second section was added. The original section was of brick, but this was covered with wood to correspond with the addition.

1775–1783–1818

Colonel Nicholas Gilman, Sr., was distinguished as the financier of New Hampshire in the Revolution. He was chosen Treasurer and Receiver General of the State in 1775 and served as such until his death in 1783, when he was succeeded by his eldest son, Honorable John Taylor Gilman. He was also Continental Loan Officer, a leading member of the State Committee of Safety from 1777 to 1779, and Councillor of the

State from 1777 to the day of his death. "Colonel Gilman's relation to the financial affairs of New Hampshire is said to have been much as that of Robert Morris to those of the Nation, and he managed them with the same prudence and skill."

In his capacity of Treasurer of the State, Colonel Gilman had his office in this house and there affixed his signature to the paper bills of credit to which the State and Country were obliged to resort to carry on the war.

His active duties as officer of the State did not, however, prevent him from devoting a part of his time to the military service, and he held the commission of Colonel of the Fourth Regiment of Militia throughout the war. As such he commanded a detachment from his regiment which joined General Whipple's brigade with the Northern Continental Army at Saratoga and aided in the capture of General Burgoyne. At the same time he was First Lieutenant of the Independent Company of Light Infantry that volunteered and marched to Saratoga in 1777 under command of its captain, Colonel John Langdon, afterwards Governor of New Hampshire, first President pro tem. of the United States Senate and a Signer of the Constitution.

Within the walls of this mansion were born his children, three of whom became conspicuous and illustrious figures in the history of the State.

Honorable John Taylor Gilman, the eldest son of Colonel Nicholas Gilman, Sr., was born in the old house in 1753, and upon the death of his parents took up his residence there, remaining until 1818, when he removed to the dwelling on the south side of Front Street.

It was during his tenancy, that the street upon which the house is situated received the designation of "Governor's Lane."

On the morning after the battle of Lexington he marched with that heroic band of one hundred volunteers from Rockingham County to Cambridge, and was chosen Sergeant of Captain James Hackett's Company. He afterwards became assistant to his father, Treasurer Gilman. In 1779 he was elected a member of the New Hampshire Legislature, was a delegate to the Convention at Hartford, Connecticut, called to take measures for the common defence in 1780, and a member of the State Committee of Safety in 1781 and 1782. In 1782 he was elected a member of Congress, and the following year succeeded his father as State Treasurer and served until 1786, and again from 1791 to 1794, when he was elected Governor of New Hampshire, to which office he was re-elected until 1805, and again elected Governor in 1813-1814 and 1815. In 1814 the military defences required his exclusive attention, and at the alarm of Portsmouth he took command in person of a large detachment of militia, which was stationed by his order in that vicinity. In this connection it is interesting to note that two of Governor Gilman's Aides were members of the New Hampshire Society of the Cincinnati, Colonel Daniel Gookin, an original member and Secretary of the Society, and Colonel Bradbury Cilley, in right of his father, General Joseph Cilley, an original member and President of the Society.

Another son, destined to become most illustrious in the history of his country, was born here August 3, 1755. This son was Captain the Honorable Nicholas Gilman, Jr., who resided with his brother, Governor John Taylor Gilman. At the age of twenty-one he was made Adjutant of the Third Regiment New Hampshire Continental Line, and in 1778 became the senior Deputy Adjutant-General of the Continental Army, on the staff of General Washington, serving in that capacity with great credit, until the close of the war, participating in all of the important battles and campaigns in which, under Washington, the chief part of the army was engaged.

In 1787 Captain Gilman and John Langdon were chosen delegates to the Federal Convention of States, which assembled in Philadelphia, and framed and adopted the Constitution and, the delegates signing in the order of States, the signatures of Langdon and Gilman followed immediately after that of General Washington, as President of the Convention. Captain Gilman enjoyed the distinction of being one of the youngest, if not the youngest, of the members of that distinguished body which, as Chancellor Kent wrote, " combined a very rare union of the best talents, experience, information, patriotism, probity and character which the country afforded."

After the adoption of the Constitution he was a member of Congress from 1789 to 1797. In 1804-1805 he was a member of the New Hampshire State Senate, and on March 4, 1805, was elected to the United States Senate, and served continuously until his death at Philadelphia, May 3, 1814.

Captain Gilman was an original member of the New Hampshire Society of the Cincinnati and a delegate to the General Meetings in 1787 and 1790.

Upon his death the Society adopted Resolutions and the members wore " black crepe on the left arm for thirty days, as a badge of respect and esteem they have for his memory."

1818-1824

A third son, Colonel the Honorable Nathaniel Gilman, succeeded his father in the treasury department — the Continental Loan Office — as early as 1783. In 1795-1796 and again in 1802-1803 he was a member of the State Senate, and in 1805 became State Treasurer, a position which his father and eldest brother had so acceptably filled before him, and served until 1809, and again from 1811 to 1814.

From 1818 to 1824 the old mansion was occupied by Captain Nathaniel Gilman, son of Colonel the Honorable Nathaniel Gilman and grandson of Colonel the Honorable Nicholas Gilman, Sr. Captain Gilman was a very prominent citizen of Exeter and a large landed proprietor. When the British fleet cruised in dangerous proximity to the coast of New Hampshire, Captain Gilman marched to Portsmouth in command of his company of the Fourth Regiment. Captain Gilman married, November 6, 1817, Elizabeth Gardiner of Philadelphia, and several of his children were born within the walls of the " Gilman House," among them being Honorable John Gardiner Gilman, the present President of the New Hampshire Society of the Cincinnati. In 1824 Captain Gilman removed to the house on High Street, which was afterwards his home.

1824-1903

From the year 1824 to the present date the house has been occupied by different branches of the family, descendants of Colonel Nicholas Gilman, Sr., with the exception of the years 1881 to 1883, when it was owned by Mr. J. Van Schaick, of whom it was purchased by the late Mr. John Taylor Perry, a great-grandson of Colonel Nicholas Gilman, Sr., who restored it to its original condition. On November 1, 1902, the house was purchased of the executors of the estate, by the New Hampshire Society of the Cincinnati, for its permanent headquarters. Truly, no more fitting memorial of the Revolutionary days could have been found.

Here met the most distinguished military and political characters of the Revolutionary period, notably General Sullivan, General Nathaniel Folsom, Meshech Weare, many members of the New Hampshire Cincinnati, the Provincial Congress, the Committee of Safety of New Hampshire, and within its walls many honored sons of New Hampshire have been entertained, including Daniel Webster, who was frequently a guest while attending the sessions of the court in Exeter.

The house itself is in an excellent state of preservation. The partially panelled walls, the quaint windows with wide sills, the large and cheerful fireplaces in which the original "dogs" still do duty are all interesting and attractive, and relate distinctively to Colonial days. The room in which Treasurer Gilman transacted the important business of State has ever since been known as "The Office." A quaint place indeed is this old-time workroom. With high, small windows fitted with wooden shutters, showing the great thickness of the house wall, and well-built fireplace, one is impressed with the solidity and sense of security of the surroundings.

Within but a few moments' walk are located the beautiful buildings of the Phillips Exeter Academy, the Hotel Squamscott, the Post Office, the Folsom Tavern, where Washington was entertained and the New Hampshire Society of the Cincinnati was organized, the "Garrison" house built in 1650, and the site of General Enoch Poor's home.

A Brief History of the Society
OF THE CINCINNATI AS FORMED BY THE OFFICERS OF THE AMERICAN ARMY AT THE CONCLUSION OF THE REVOLUTIONARY WAR, 1783

THE historic and time-honored Society of the Cincinnati was instituted May 13, 1783, by the officers of the Continental Army then in cantonment at Newburgh, on the Hudson River. Major-General Baron de Steuben presided over the convention of officers, at which the institution of the Order was adopted, the governing principles of which are as follows:

"It having pleased the Supreme Governor of the Universe, in the disposition of human affairs, to cause the separation of the Colonies of North America from the domination of Great Britain and, after a bloody conflict of eight years, to establish them free, independent and sovereign States, connected, by alliances founded on reciprocal advantages, with some of the great princes and powers of the earth.

"To perpetuate, therefore, as well the remembrance of this vast event, as the mutual friendships which have been formed under the pressure of common danger, and in many instances cemented by the blood of the parties, the officers of the American Army do hereby, in the most solemn manner, associate, constitute and combine themselves into One Society of Friends, to endure as long as they shall endure, or any of their eldest male posterity, and, in failure thereof, the collateral branches, who may be judged worthy of becoming its supporters and members.

"The officers of the American Army, having generally been taken from the citizens of America, possess high veneration for the character of that illustrious Roman, LUCIUS QUINTIUS CINCINNATUS; and being resolved to follow his example, by returning to their citizenship, they think they may with propriety denominate themselves

The Society of the Cincinnati

"The following principles shall be immutable and form the basis of the Society of the Cincinnati:

"An incessant attention to preserve inviolate those exalted rights and liberties of human nature for which they have fought and bled, and without which the high rank of a rational being is a curse instead of a blessing.

"An unalterable determination to promote and cherish, between the respective States, that union and national honor so essentially necessary to their happiness, and the future dignity of the American empire.

"To render permanent the cordial affection subsisting among the officers. This spirit will dictate brotherly kindness in all things, and particularly extend to the most substantial acts of beneficence, according to the ability of the Society, towards those officers and their families who unfortunately may be under the necessity of receiving it."

For convenience the Society was divided into thirteen State Societies, and upon the roll of original members appeared the names of nearly all of the historic military and naval characters of the Revolution. The General Society composed of the general officers and delegates from each State Society was required to meet every three years, and State Societies annually on July 4th.

The first meeting of the General Society was held at Philadelphia, May 4, 1784, when the first general officers were elected: His Excellency General George Washington, of Virginia, President General; Major-General Horatio Gates, of Virginia, Vice-President General; Major-General Henry Knox, of Massachusetts, Secretary General; Brigadier-General Otho Holland Williams, of Maryland, Assistant Secretary General; Major-General Alexander MacDougall, of New York, Treasurer General. General Washington served as President General until his decease in 1799.

The insignia of the Society was designed by Major L'Enfant, of the French Corps of Engineers, who planned the city of Washington, and is an enamelled gold eagle, displayed, bearing on its breast medallions charged with the emblems of the Order, and the motto, *Omnia Relinquit Servare Rempublicam*, suspended from a light-blue ribbon edged with white, emblematic of the union between France and America. A highly treasured relic in the possession of the Society is the insignia richly set in diamonds, presented in 1784 by the French naval officers through Admiral Count D'Estaing to General Washington, by whom it was worn, and has since been regularly transmitted to each of his successors as President General.

In France, where the French officers formed an organization under the presidency of the Count D'Estaing, the Cincinnati reached a most eminent distinction, including among its members the most illustrious nobles and military officers of France.

Many of the French officers valued the Order of the Cincinnati more highly than the Cross of St. Louis, and the Society was organized with the consent of the King, Louis XVI, in Council, who by decree, granted special permission to the French Cincinnati to wear the order, an exceptional privilege, since no other foreign order was allowed to be worn in France except that of the Golden Fleece.

As the oldest military order in America, inspired by sentiments of patriotism, worthy of the men who achieved American independence, the Society of the Cincinnati has ever maintained an honored position and its eagle has become a treasured heirloom in many American families.

The New Hampshire Society

THE New Hampshire Society of the Cincinnati was organized November 18, 1783, at Folsom's Tavern in Exeter, under the direction of Major-General John Sullivan, who became its first President. Many of the leading officers of the New Hampshire Continental Line became original members of the New Hampshire Society, including General Henry Dearborn, General James Reed, Colonel Joseph Cilley, Captain Nicholas Gilman and Captain Jonathan Cass, father of the eminent statesman, Lewis Cass. The New Hampshire Society has ever occupied a distinguished position in the Order, and chiefly to its efforts in 1784 in opposing the proposed amendment to the institution, abolishing the rule of hereditary succession, is due the preservation of the Order to posterity. The New Hampshire Society holds its annual meetings at its headquarters in Exeter on July 4th, and in addition holds special meetings to commemorate other historic events in the Revolution.

Rules for Admission of Members

ELIGIBILITY.

By the institution the officers entitled to become members of the Society were declared to be as follows:

"All the officers of the American Army, as well (1) those who have resigned with honor after three years' service in the capacity of officers, or (2) who have been deranged by the Resolutions of Congress upon the several reforms of the army, or (3) those who have continued to the end of the war, have the right to become parties to this institution; provided that they subscribe one month's pay, and sign their names to the general rules in their respective State Societies, those who are present with the army immediately and others within six months after the army shall be disbanded, extraordinary cases excepted; the rank, time of service, resolution of Congress by which any may have been deranged, and place of residence must be added to each name; and as a testimony of affection to the memory and the offspring of such officers as have died in the service, their eldest male branches have the same right of becoming members as the children of the actual members of the Society."

The officers who were elected members of the Society under the institution as above given, became the original members of the Society.

In 1854 the General Society passed the following resolution, making descendants of officers who did not become original members eligible to membership:

"*Resolved*, That each State Society shall have the full right and power to regulate the admission of members, both as to the qualifications of the members and the terms of admission; provided, that admission be confined to the male descendants of original members, or of those who are now members (including collateral branches as contemplated by the original constitution); or to the male descendants of such officers of the army or navy as may have been entitled to admission, but who failed to avail themselves thereof within the time limited by the constitution; or to male descendants of such officers of the army or navy of the Revolution as may have resigned with honor or left the service with reputation; or to the male collateral relatives of any officers who died in service without leaving issue."

Every applicant to be eligible must have either the qualifications stated in the institution or under the Rule of 1854.

The succession and admission to membership in the New Hampshire Society descends from the ancestor, who was an officer, in the eldest male line to the eldest male descendant, according to the rules of primogeniture at the common law.

Only one person at a time shall be competent to be elected as the hereditary representative of an officer, who was either an original member, or who was entitled to become an original member of the Society, according to the Rule of 1854.

The following rules and principles are ordinarily observed in considering applications:

I. Direct descendants shall be preferred to collaterals.

II. Among direct descendants the male line is to be preferred to the female line.

III. When the direct male line is extinct, and there are

male descendants through intervening female lines, the Society may select the representative from among such male descendants.

IV. When there are no direct descendants the eldest collateral branch is chosen, according to the rules of primogeniture at the common law.

V. The claims of descendants in the female line shall be determined according to the same rules which govern priority in the male line, so far as applicable.

VI. Waivers from those having prior rights to the applicant may be accepted, and the failure of any eligible person having knowledge of the existence of his claim to apply within a reasonable time may be treated as a waiver thereof.

VII. Where a vacancy has existed for many years, or the officer has never been represented, the Society may select a representative from among the descendants.

The right of admission and succession to membership is not absolute, but subject to the judgment of the Society, as to whether the applicant is deemed "worthy of becoming its supporter and member." The law of inheritance confers only the privilege to be voted for, and the Society reserves the right to choose such one as seems to it best fitted to promote its ends, according to the institution.

ADMISSION FEE.

When the Society was instituted in 1783 each officer, who became an original member, paid an admission fee of one month's pay, which constituted the Permanent Fund. Therefore, each State Society makes it a condition precedent, that every applicant whose ancestor was not an original member shall, upon admission, pay a sum equivalent to what his ancestor should have paid, had he become an original member, with interest, which sum is averaged and commuted in many of the State Societies at a fee of $500.00, and in the New Hampshire Society at $250.00.

The admission fee of $250.00 to the New Hampshire Society is an endowed fee in perpetuity. There are no annual dues.

Officers and Committees, 1902-03

President
Hon. JOHN GARDINER GILMAN

Vice-President
JOHN HARVEY TREAT

Secretary
FREDERICK BACON PHILBROOK

Treasurer
FRANKLIN SENTER FRISBIE

Assistant Treasurer
HENRY DEXTER WARREN

Chaplain
Rt. Rev. JOHN HAZEN WHITE, D.D.

Standing Executive Committee
FREDERICK BACON PHILBROOK, *Chairman*
HENRY DEXTER WARREN, *Committee Secretary*
Hon. JOHN GARDINER GILMAN
JOHN HARVEY TREAT
FRANKLIN SENTER FRISBIE
FRANCIS OLCOTT ALLEN
JAMES WILLIAM SULLIVAN
FRANKLIN THOMASON BEATTY, M.D.

Member of the Standing Executive Committee of the General Society
FRANCIS OLCOTT ALLEN

Delegates to the General Society
Hon. JOHN GARDINER GILMAN
Rt. Rev. JOHN HAZEN WHITE, D.D.
SAMUEL LORD MORISON
FRANCIS OLCOTT ALLEN
FREDERICK BACON PHILBROOK

Alternates to the General Society
JOHN WILLIAM ADAMS
JOHN M. GLIDDEN
JAMES WILLIAM SULLIVAN
FRANKLIN SENTER FRISBIE
WILLIAM LITHGOW WILLEY, Sc.D.

Committee on Membership
FRANCIS OLCOTT ALLEN, *Chairman*
FRANKLIN SENTER FRISBIE, *Committee Secretary*
FREDERICK BACON PHILBROOK

Members

Mr. JOHN WILLIAM ADAMS
    Former Representative to the General Court of Massachusetts

Mr. FRANCIS OLCOTT ALLEN
    Member Standing Executive Committee of the General Society

Mr. WILLIAM TURNER BACON, A.M., M.D.

Mr. GEORGE CARLETON BEAL

Mr. FRANKLIN THOMASON BEATTY, M.D.

Mr. DAVID LANE BILLINGS, A.B.

Hon. JONATHAN PRINCE CILLEY, A.B.
    Late Colonel and Brevet Brigadier-General U. S. Volunteers
    Former Representative to the General Court of Maine

Mr. JOSEPH CILLEY

Mr. JAMES MILNOR COIT, A.M., PH.D.
    Assistant Rector, St. Paul's School, Concord

Hon. STEPHEN MOODY CROSBY, A.B.
    Late Major and Brevet Lieutenant-Colonel U. S. Volunteers
    Former Judge Advocate General (Brigadier-General), State of Massachusetts

Mr. FRANKLIN SENTER FRISBIE, LL.B.

Mr. ROBERT SPEAR FOGG

Mr. BRADLEY LUTHER FRYE

Hon. JOHN GARDINER GILMAN
    Former Representative to General Court of New Hampshire

Mr. JOHN M. GLIDDEN
    Former Lieutenant-Colonel and A.D.C., State of Maine

Mr. CHARLES HENRI GOOKIN

Hon. ETHAN ALLEN HITCHCOCK
    Secretary of the Interior of the U. S.

Hon. HENRY OAKES KENT, A.M., LL.D.
    Late Colonel U. S. Volunteers
    Former U. S. Naval Officer of the Port of Boston
    President New Hampshire Forrestry Commission

Mr. GEORGE BRIDGE LEIGHTON, A.B.

Mr. HORACE PRESCOTT MCCLARY
    Former Representative to the General Court of Vermont

Mr. IRA DARLING MCCLARY *
    Late Lieutenant U. S. Volunteers
    Former U. S. Consular Agent, Province of Quebec

* Honorary Member.

Mr. JOHN MCGAFFEY, A.B.
Mr. HORACE MORISON, A.B.
Mr. SAMUEL LORD MORISON, A.B.
Mr. CHARLES CASS MUNRO
Mr. JOHN STRONG PENNIMAN
Hon. THOMAS PITTS *
Mr. FREDERICK BACON PHILBROOK
Mr. JOSEPH VILA PRICHARD, A.B.
Rev. JEREMIAH EAMES RANKIN, D.D., LL.D.
 President of Howard University, Washington, D. C.
Mr. EDWARD ADOLPHUS ROLLINS
Mr. WILLIAM DAVIS SAWYER, A.B., LL.B.
 Former Quartermaster-General (Brigadier-General) State of New Hampshire
Mr. ALFRED LEE SHAPLEIGH
 Director International Exposition of St. Louis
Mr. NATHAN PARKER SHORTRIDGE *
Mr. JOHN HENRY SHORTRIDGE
Mr. SAMUEL STRONG SPAULDING
Mr. CHARLES WALTER STEWART
Mr. JAMES WILLIAM SULLIVAN
Mr. HOBART CHATFIELD CHATFIELD-TAYLOR, A.B.
 Knight of the Royal Order of Isabella of Spain
Mr. FREDERICK DIODATI THOMPSON, LL.B.
 Chevalier of the Imperial Order of the Medjidie
 Chevalier of the Imperial Order of Osmanlie
Mr. JOHN HARVEY TREAT, A.M.
Mr. WILLIAM FRANKLIN TRUFANT
Mr. HENRY DEXTER WARREN
 Lieutenant 5th Regiment Massachusetts Infantry
Mr. WILLIAM BOERUM WETMORE
 Late Lieutenant U. S. Army
Rt. Rev. JOHN HAZEN WHITE, D.D.
 Bishop of Indiana, District of Michigan City
 General Chaplain of the Order of the Cincinnati
Mr. WILLIAM LITHGOW WILLEY, Sc. D.
 Captain and Quartermaster A. & H. A. Co.

*Honorary Member

HONORABLE NICHOLAS GILMAN
SON OF HONORABLE NICHOLAS AND ANN
(TAYLOR) GILMAN,
BORN AT EXETER, NEW HAMPSHIRE,
AUGUST THIRD, 1755,
IN THE FAMOUS OLD GILMAN HOUSE
NOW KNOWN AS
CINCINNATI MEMORIAL HALL.
CAPTAIN & SENIOR DEPUTY ADJUTANT-GENERAL
OF THE CONTINENTAL ARMY
ON THE STAFF OF GENERAL WASHINGTON.
MEMBER OF THE CONTINENTAL CONGRESS & ONE OF
THE FRAMERS AND A SIGNER OF THE
CONSTITUTION OF THE UNITED STATES.
MEMBER OF THE UNITED STATES SENATE
FOR MORE THAN NINE YEARS AND UNTIL HIS DECEASE,
AT PHILADELPHIA, MAY THIRD, 1814.
AN ORIGINAL MEMBER OF THE NEW HAMPSHIRE
SOCIETY OF THE CINCINNATI
AND A
DELEGATE TO THE GENERAL SOCIETY.

Nich Gilman

Officers of the General Society, 1902-05

President General
Hon. WINSLOW WARREN
Massachusetts Society

Vice-President General
Hon. JAMES SIMONS, LL.D.
South Carolina Society

Secretary General
Hon. ASA BIRD GARDINER, LL.D., L.H.D.
Rhode Island Society

Treasurer General
Hon. FREDERICK WOLCOTT JACKSON
New Jersey Society

Assistant Treasurer General
Hon. JOHN CROPPER
Virginia Society

Standing Executive Committee

ASA BIRD GARDINER, LL.D., L.H.D., *Rhode Island Society*, Chairman
JAMES SIMONS, LL.D., *South Carolina Society*
FRANCIS MARINUS CALDWELL, *Pennsylvania Society*
OSWALD TILGHMAN, *Maryland Society*
GEORGE BLISS SANDFORD, U. S. A., *Connecticut Society*
CHARLES UPHAM BELL, *Massachusetts Society*
TALBOT OLYPHANT, *New York Society*
JOHN CROPPER, *Virginia Society*
FRANK LANDON HUMPHREYS, S.T.D., *New Jersey Society*
FRANCIS OLCOTT ALLEN, *New Hampshire Society*
HENRY HOBART BELLAS, U. S. A., *Delaware Society*
JOHN COLLINS DAVES, *North Carolina Society*
WALTER GLASCO CHARLTON, *Georgia Society*
THE PRESIDENT GENERAL, *ex officio*

Chaplains

The Rev. MANCIUS HOLMES HUTTON, D.D.
New York Society
The Rev. FRANK LANDON HUMPHREYS, S.T.D.
New Jersey Society
The Rt. Rev. JOHN HAZEN WHITE, D.D.
New Hampshire Society

A List of the Presidents, Vice-Presidents, and Secretaries of the State Societies of the Cincinnati

NEW HAMPSHIRE
President, JOHN GARDINER GILMAN
Vice-President, JOHN HARVEY TREAT
Secretary, FREDERICK BACON PHILBROOK

MASSACHUSETTS
President, WINSLOW WARREN
Vice-President, THORNTON KIRKLAND LOTHROP
Secretary, DAVID GREENE HASKINS, Jr.

RHODE ISLAND
President, ASA BIRD GARDINER, LL.D.
Vice-President, JAMES M. VARNUM
Secretary, GEORGE WASHINGTON OLNEY

CONNECTICUT
President, GEORGE BLISS SANDFORD, U. S. A.
Vice-President, HENRY LARCOM ABBOT, U. S. A.
Secretary, MORRIS WOODRUFF SEYMOUR

NEW YORK
President, Vacancy
Vice-President, TALBOT OLYPHANT
Secretary, FRANCIS KEY PENDLETON

NEW JERSEY

President, Frank Landon Humphreys, S.T.D.
Vice-President, Franklin Davenport Howell
Secretary, Wessel Ten Broeck Stout Imlay

PENNSYLVANIA

President, Richard Dale
Vice-President, Francis Marinus Caldwell
Secretary, William Macpherson Hornor

DELAWARE

President, Thomas David Pearce
Vice-President, John Patten Wales
Secretary, Henry Hobart Bellas, U. S. A.

MARYLAND

President, Otho Holland Williams
Vice-President, William Henry De Courcy, M.D.
Secretary, Thomas Edward Sears, M.D.

VIRGINIA

President, John Cropper
Vice-President, George Ben Johnston, M.D.
Secretary, Patrick Henry Carey Cabell

NORTH CAROLINA

President, Wilson Gray Lamb
Vice-President, Vacancy
Secretary, Charles Luken Davis, U. S. A.

SOUTH CAROLINA

President, James Simons, LL.D.
Vice-President, Daniel Elliott Huger Smith
Secretary, Henry Massingberd Tucker, Jr.

GEORGIA

President, Walter Glasco Charlton
Vice-President, Vacancy
Secretary, George Noble Jones

CPSIA information can be obtained
at www.ICGtesting.com
Printed in the USA
BVHW041714031218
534659BV00016B/892/P